design and illustration by
Felicia Norton & Charles Smith

AF104568

Copyright 2024 by TwoSeasJoinPress
ISBN 978-1-7363254-1-4

All proceeds from the sale of this book support the Hope Project India. The Hope Project India (In US: https://childrensashramfund.org/, in Europe or Asia: https://hopeproject.nl) provides food, education and health care to those in need in the Nizamuddin Basti area of Delhi, India. It was founded by Pir Vilayat Inayat Khan, the son of this book's author, Hazrat Inayat Khan.

The Fairy's Dream

There is a story that can explain the mystery of life's purpose. A fairy had a great desire to amuse herself, and she descended on the earth.

And there children had made a little doll's-house. She wanted to enter this doll's-house, but it was difficult for her to enter into the space where only a doll can go.

'Very well', she said, 'I am going to try a different way. I will send one finger by this way, and another finger by another way, and each part by different ways.'

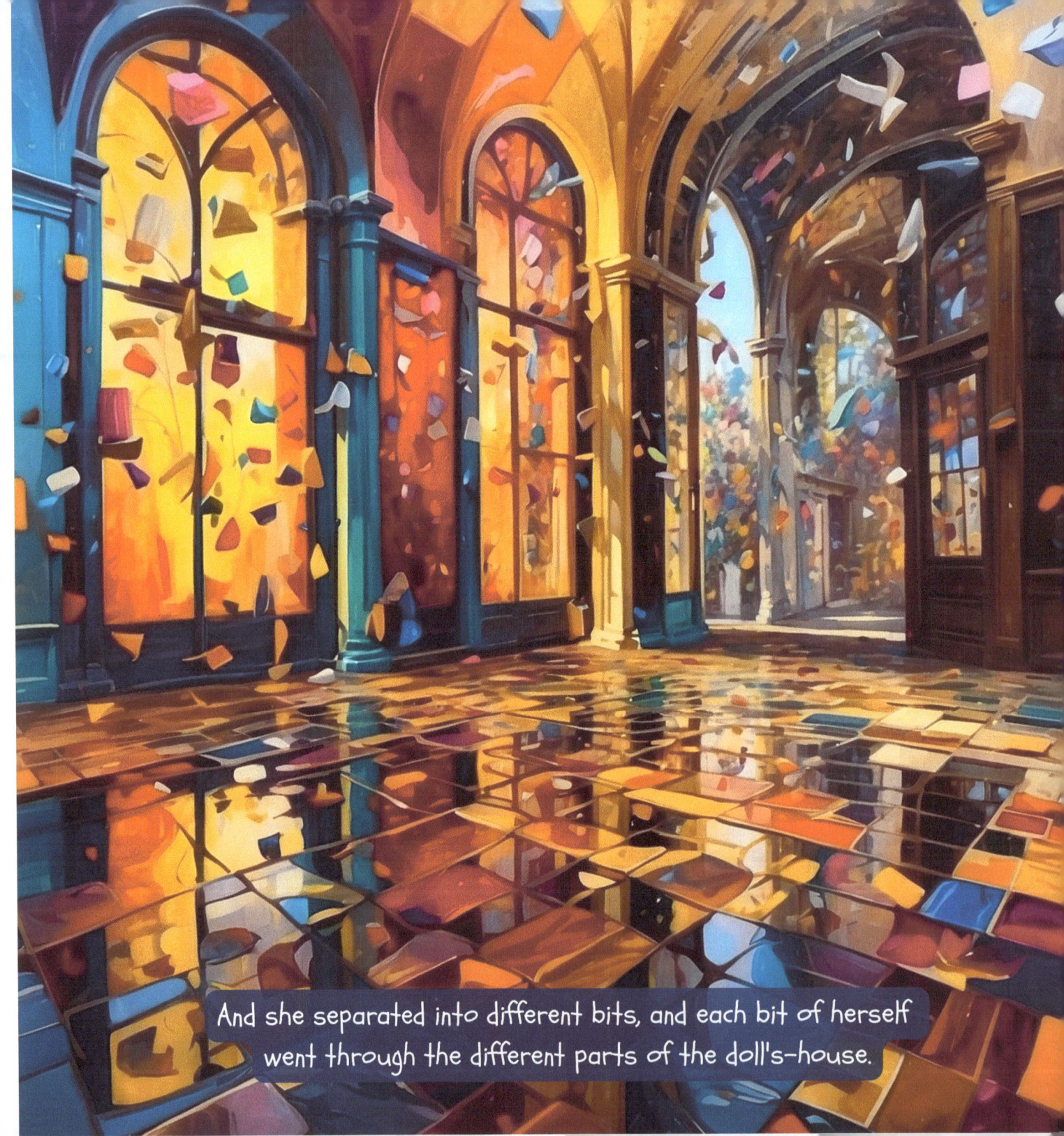

And she separated into different bits, and each bit of herself went through the different parts of the doll's-house.

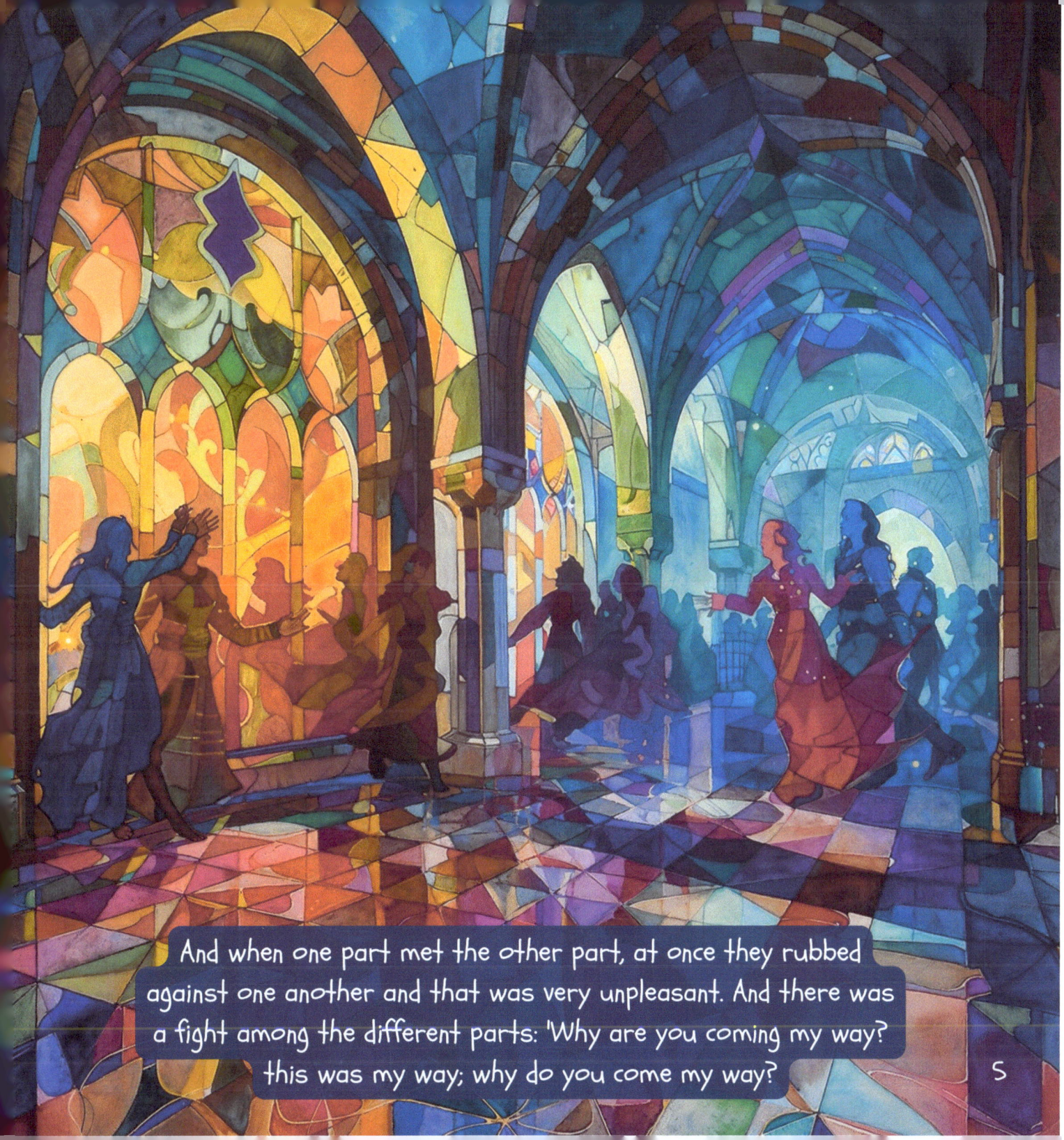

And when one part met the other part, at once they rubbed against one another and that was very unpleasant. And there was a fight among the different parts: 'Why are you coming my way? this was my way; why do you come my way?'

Each part of the fairy's being interested itself in something, in some part of that doll's-house. When that moment of interest passed, a certain part of her being wanted to go out of the doll's-house.

But then there were other parts of the being which were not willing to let it go. They were holding it: 'You stay here; you cannot go out.' Some parts of her being wanted to push out another part, but there was no way of putting it out.

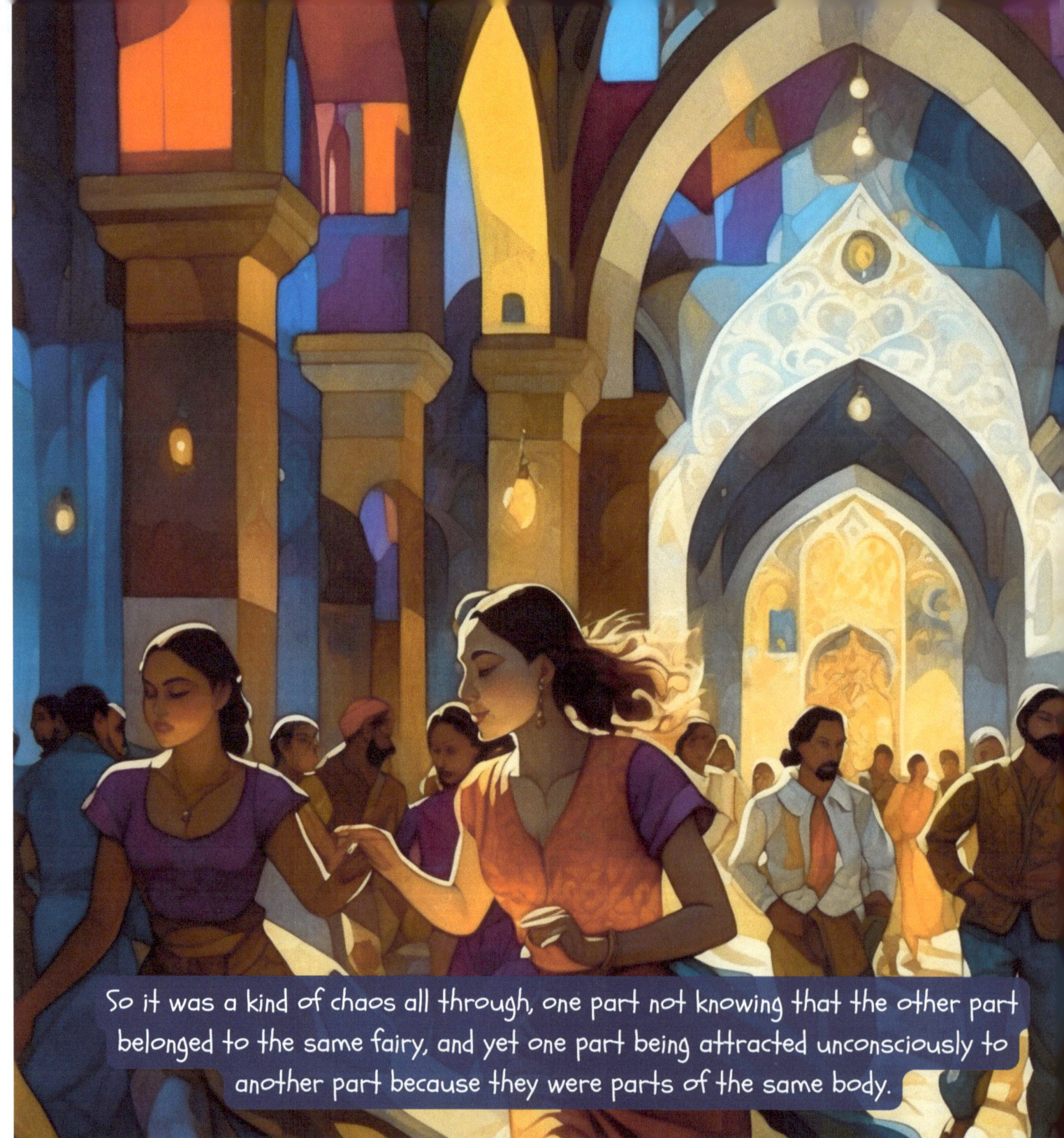

In the end the heart of the fairy moved about also. This heart soothed every other part, saying, 'You have come from me. I wish to console, I wish to serve you. If you are troubled, I wish to take away your trouble. If you are in need of a service, I wish to render it you. If you lack anything, I wish to bring it for you. I know how much you are troubled in this doll's-house.'

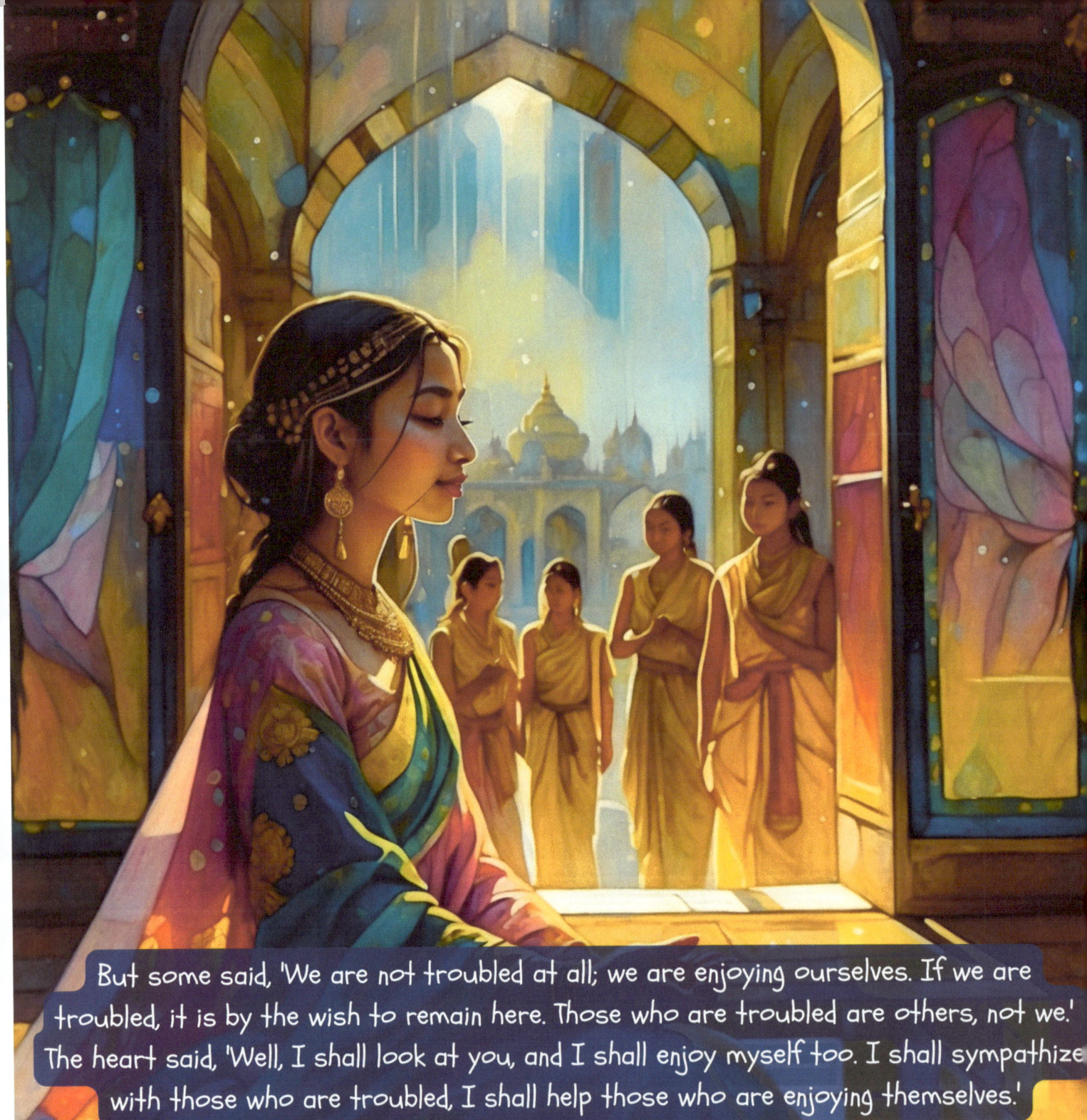

But some said, 'We are not troubled at all; we are enjoying ourselves. If we are troubled, it is by the wish to remain here. Those who are troubled are others, not we.' The heart said, 'Well, I shall look at you, and I shall enjoy myself too. I shall sympathize with those who are troubled, I shall help those who are enjoying themselves.'

This was the one part of the fairy's being which was conscious of its atoms scattered all around. But the atoms were hardly conscious of it, although since they belonged to the same body, they were attracted to the heart, knowingly or unknowingly, consciously or unconsciously.

Such was the power of the heart. It was just like the power of the sun, that turns the responsive flower into a sun-flower.

And so the power of the heart of the fairy turned every part of its being that responded, into a heart. And as the heart was light and life itself, the doll's-house could no longer hold the heart. The heart was experiencing the joy of the doll's house, but was at the same time able to fly away

The heart was delighted to find all its atoms belonging to its body, and it worked through all and through every part of its organs; so, in time, it turned every part of its organs into a heart also, by which this phenomenon was fulfilled.

God is love, if God is Love, Love is too sacred, and to utter this word without meaning is a vain repetition. A person to whom it means something, her lips close, she can say little. For Love is a revelation in itself; no study is necessary, no meditation is needed, no piety is required.

If Love is pure, if the spark of love has begun to twinkle, then the person need not go somewhere to gain spirituality, then spirituality is within herself.

One must keep blowing the spark till it turns into a perpetual fire. The fire worshippers of old did not worship a fire which went out. They worshiped a perpetual fire. Where is that perpetual fire to be found? In one's own heart.

The spark that one finds glowing for a moment and that then becomes dim, it does not belong to heaven, for in heaven all things are lasting. It must belong to some other place. Love has become a word from the dictionary, a word which is used 1000 times in the day, which means nothing.

To the one who knows what love means, love means patience, love means endurance, love means tolerance, love means sacrifice, love means service. All things such as gentleness, humility, modesty, graciousness, kindness all are the different manifestations of love.

It is the same to say God is all and all is God and to say Love is all and all is love. And it is to find it, to feel it, and to experience its warmth and to see in the world the light of love and to keep its glow, and to hold love's flame high as a sacred torch, to guide one in one's life journey it is in this that the purpose of life is fulfilled.

According to the common standard of life a person with common sense is counted to be the right person a fit person. But from a mystical standard that person alone can begin to be the right person who is beginning to feel sympathy with her fellow human beings. For by the study of philosophy, mysticism, by the practices of concentration and meditation, to what do we attain? To a capability that would enable us to serve our fellow human beings better.

Friends, truth is simple, but for the very reason that it is simple, the souls will not take it, because our life on earth is such that everything we value, we have to pay a great price for it to get it. And one thinks that if truth is most precious of all things, then one thinks that, how can truth be attained most simply? It is this illusion that makes everyone deny a simple truth and search for complexity.

There are two things: knowing and being. It is easy to know the truth but most difficult to be the truth. It is not in knowing the truth that life's purpose is accomplished. Life's purpose is accomplished in being truth.

Hazrat Inayat Khan

The tale and commentary here are adapted from several sources of the lectures and writings of Hazrat Inayat Khan.

www.ingramcontent.com/pod-product-compliance
Lightning Source LLC
LaVergne TN
LVHW071654060526
838200LV00029B/455